With love to all my sleepers big and small: Joe, Fiona, Avery and Myrtle. And my dad for the rhyming skills. And my mom for the ability to be productive at 4 a.m.
-C.O.

To my parents for enduring all the years of my childhood insomnia. -S.W.

You can sleep in different places.
Get some rest, no matter what the case is.

Some people sleep while they float.
Lulled to sleep by a rocking boat.

Some people sleep and then work at night.

Some people sleep under the pale moonlight.

Some people sleep up in the air.

Some people sleep while at the fair.

Some people sleep in a hotel bed.

Some people sleep where the chickens are fed.

You can sleep in a crib or a bed or a bunk.

You can sleep during the day under the porch like a skunk.

You can sleep at the house of a friend or close buddy.

You can sleep on your books if you're too tired to study.

Let's take an example from the doggies you see.
You can sleep on the couch or under a tree.

You might find it ~~hard~~ fun to sleep in a new place.
Like at grandma's house, or a trip into space.

You can sleep at the movies where it's nice and dark.

You can sleep in the car and wake up when you park.

But when your body needs sleep and it's time to rest,
Just take some deep breaths and give it your best.

Let your body relax and your breathing get deep.
And wherever you are, you will fall fast asleep.

Sweet dreams!

Staci Wolfson and Carly Ornstein have been friends since they were five years old (pictured above attending a sleepover circa 1994).

Nowadays, Carly writes children's books at 4 a.m. when her children are not sleeping, obsessively researches her genealogy and tries to improve the world through public health.
www.carlyornsteinconsulting.com
Staci works in higher-education publishing and in her free time she runs a women's health support group, exercises, talks to her pets and explores new pastries with her husband, Scott.
https://substack.com/staciwolfson

The End

ISBN: 9798866647996
Copyright 2023

Made in United States
North Haven, CT
22 November 2023